TEAM SPIRIT ®

SMART BOOKS FOR YOUNG FANS

THE NEW YORK METS

BY
MARK STEWART

NORWOOD HOUSE 🏠 PRESS
CHICAGO, ILLINOIS

Norwood House Press
P.O. Box 316598
Chicago, Illinois 60631

For information regarding Norwood House Press, please visit our website at:
www.norwoodhousepress.com or call 866-565-2900.

All photos courtesy of Getty Images except the following:
New York Daily News (7),
Topps, Inc. (15, 16, 25, 34 top, 35 bottom left, 36, 42 bottom left and bottom right),
SportsChrome (4, 10, 11, 12, 14),
Black Book Partners Archives (9, 20, 21, 22, 23 bottom, 34 bottom right, 35 top, 35 bottom right, 37, 45),
Author's Collection (27, 33, 34 bottom left, 40, 41, 42 top, 43 left),
Fleer Corp. (38), Matt Richman (48).

The memorabilia and artifacts pictured in this book are presented for educational and informational purposes,
and come from the collection of the author.

Editor: Mike Kennedy
Designer: Ron Jaffe
Project Management: Black Book Partners, LLC.
Special thanks to Topps, Inc.

Library of Congress Cataloging-in-Publication Data

Stewart, Mark, 1960-
  The New York Mets / by Mark Stewart.
    p. cm. -- (Team spirit)
  Includes bibliographical references and index.
  Summary: "A Team Spirit Baseball edition featuring the New York Mets that
chronicles the history and accomplishments of the team. Includes access to
the Team Spirit website, which provides additional information, updates and
photos"--Provided by publisher.
  ISBN 978-1-59953-489-3 (library : alk. paper) -- ISBN 978-1-60357-369-6 (ebook)
  1. New York Mets (Baseball team)--History--Juvenile literature.
  I. Title.
  GV875.N45S74 2012
  796.357'64097471--dc23
                                        2011047974

Manufactured in the United States of America in North Mankato, Minnesota.
196N—012012

COVER PHOTO: The Mets celebrate a win during the 2011 season.

TABLE OF CONTENTS

ABOUT OUR GLOSSARY

In this book, there may be several words that you are reading for the first time. Some are sports words, some are new vocabulary words, and some are familiar words that are used in an unusual way. All of these words are defined on page 46. Throughout the book, sports words appear in **bold type**. Regular vocabulary words appear in ***bold italic type***.

MEET THE METS

I n baseball, the defense controls the action. No play can start until the pitcher throws the ball. That explains why the New York Mets have always built their teams around pitching. Of course, even the best pitcher needs good fielders behind him. Over the years, the Mets have also found some of baseball's fastest and finest "glove men."

Mets fans cheer as loudly for a great pitch or *sparkling* defensive play as they do for a solid hit. The players know this. In fact, they appreciate how well the fans understand baseball. The Mets enjoy playing in a city with millions of people watching them. There may be a lot of pressure, but it is also a lot of fun.

This book tells the story of the Mets. They have had many amazing seasons—plus a few they would like to forget. Through it all, one thing has never changed. No other team comes to the ballpark each day with more smiles than the Mets.

The Mets' dugout often is as busy as the city the team plays in.

Once upon a time, New York was a three-team baseball town. The Dodgers played in Brooklyn, the Giants played in Manhattan, and the Yankees played in the Bronx. The Dodgers and Giants left for California in 1958. For four seasons, the **National League (NL)** had no teams in New York. That changed in 1962 when the NL added two new clubs, the Mets and the Houston Colt .45s (now known as the Astros). The Mets moved into the Giants' old stadium while a new one was built for the team in Queens.

In their early years, the Mets played right across the river from the Yankees, who were champions of the **American League (AL)**. In order to attract fans, the Mets used players who had once been famous in the city. These players included Gil Hodges, Duke Snider, Charlie Neal, Roger Craig, Gene Woodling, and Clem

Labine. Their manager was Casey Stengel, who had been a member of the Giants, Dodgers, and Yankees. He got help in the dugout from New York baseball legend Yogi Berra.

Other Mets who were familiar to old-time baseball fans were Richie Ashburn, Frank Thomas, Gus Bell, and Roy McMillan. Unfortunately, these players were no longer stars. The Mets were terrible on the field. In their first four seasons, they finished last each year.

Casey and "assistant manager" Yogi prepare for today's opener with Dodgers at Shea Stadium.

Even though the Mets usually lost, millions of fans still came to see them. The team made a lot of money and used it to develop talented young players. This *strategy* worked. In 1969, the Mets won the NL **pennant** and the **World Series**. The team's pitchers were the best in baseball. New York's staff included Tom Seaver, Jerry Koosman, Gary Gentry, Nolan Ryan, and Tug McGraw. Their best defensive players were Jerry Grote, Bud Harrelson, Tommie Agee, and Cleon Jones.

LEFT: Gil Hodges and Duke Snider traded their Dodgers uniforms for Mets uniforms in 1962.   **ABOVE**: The team made news when Yogi Berra joined his old Yankees manager, Casey Stengel, on the Mets in 1965.

The Mets added more good players over the next few years, including Jon Matlack, John Milner, Rusty Staub, Felix Millan, and Willie Mays. They won the pennant again in 1973 but lost the World Series to the Oakland A's.

More than 10 years passed before the Mets had another championship team. Once again, they built their club around a group of young pitchers: Dwight Gooden, Ron Darling, Sid Fernandez, Jesse Orosco, and Roger

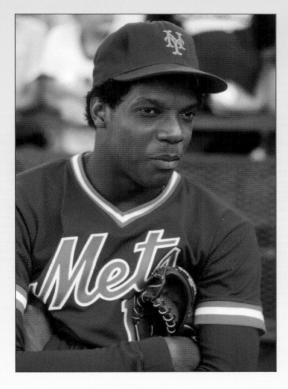

McDowell. The batting order featured experienced players such as Gary Carter, Keith Hernandez, and Ray Knight, as well as young stars Darryl Strawberry, Lenny Dykstra, and Mookie Wilson. In 1986, the Mets won their third pennant and second World Series.

In 2000, the Mets returned to the World Series. Again, they relied on strong pitchers, including Mike Hampton, Al Leiter, John Franco, and Armando Benitez. New York also had one of the best fielding teams ever. Their offense was excellent as well, thanks to stars such as Mike Piazza and Edgardo Alfonzo.

LEFT: Tom Seaver won 198 games for the Mets and helped them reach the World Series twice.   **ABOVE**: Dwight Gooden was the leader of the team's pitching staff in the 1980s.

The Mets played the Yankees for the championship that fall. It was the first time New York teams had met in the World Series since 1956. Even though the Mets lost the "Subway Series," they reminded baseball fans everywhere of the good old days, when New York City was the center of baseball almost every autumn.

In the years that followed, the Mets fielded more strong teams. The heart of these clubs was a group of talented Spanish-speaking players. Several **veteran** stars joined the team, including Johan Santana, Pedro Martinez, Carlos Delgado, and Carlos Beltran. Many fans thought Beltran was the best all-around player the Mets ever had.

LEFT: Mike Piazza waves to fans after hitting a home run.
RIGHT: Jose Reyes is ready to field a batted ball.

These experienced players helped the younger Mets learn the game. David Wright and Jose Reyes led the way. Both became All-Stars. In 2006, the Mets came very close to returning to the World Series. They lost in Game 7 of the **National League Championship Series (NLCS)**.

In 2009, the Mets opened a new stadium. It was built to favor teams with good pitching, defense, and speed. These qualities have always been important ingredients in the Mets' recipe for success. They also make for exciting baseball. When the Mets are on the field, there is almost never a dull moment.

HOME TURF

From 1964 to 2008, the Mets played at Shea Stadium. It opened at the same time as the New York World's Fair. The stadium was named after William Shea, a man who worked very hard to bring National League baseball back to New York after the Dodgers and Giants left town.

In 2009, the Mets moved into a new home, next door to Shea. The pitchers loved playing there because it was hard to hit the ball over the wall. The hitters did not like it for the same reason. After the 2011 season, the Mets lowered the height of the outfield fences and moved them closer to home plate. While these changes favored hitters, the Mets' stadium still is considered a good ballpark for pitchers.

BY THE NUMBERS

- The Mets' stadium has 41,940 seats for baseball games.
- The distance from home plate to the left field foul pole is 335 feet.
- The distance from home plate to the center field wall is 408 feet.
- The distance from home plate to the right field foul pole is 330 feet.

Fans like the Mets' new home because it has the feel of an old-time stadium.

Since their very first season, the Mets have worn uniforms with the blue of the Dodgers and the orange of the Giants. The team also reminds fans of New York's proud history with its *logo*. It was designed by a famous cartoonist named Ray Gatto. He included three important landmarks in the logo: the Empire State Building, the United Nations Building, and the Williamsburg Savings Bank, which is the tallest building in Brooklyn.

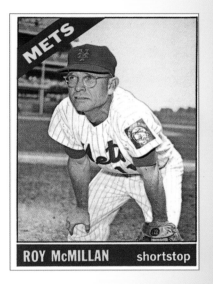

Over the years, the Mets have worn different shades and combinations of orange and blue. Sometimes for home games, the team dresses in a *pinstripe* uniform that is almost identical to the one worn in 1962. It is still one of the fans' favorites.

In 1998, the Mets added black as a team color. In 2012, the team celebrated its 50th anniversary with uniforms that looked just like the ones from 1962.

LEFT: David Wright wears the Mets' 2011 pinstripe uniform.
ABOVE: This trading card of Roy McMillan shows the team's uniform from the mid-1960s.

WE WON!

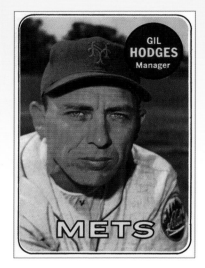

GIL HODGES
Manager

METS

When the Mets are playing for a championship, baseball fans have come to expect the unexpected. In 1969, for example, few people believed New York would win more than half their games when the season started. What were the chances of winning the World Series? Well, the Mets had never even had a winning year. It seemed impossible.

One person who believed in the Mets was their manager, Gil Hodges. He had played in seven World Series and knew exactly what it took to get there. He promised his players that if they made fewer mistakes, they could compete with any team in baseball.

The Mets were led by pitchers Tom Seaver and Jerry Koosman. They were very young and very good. Seaver won 25 games and Koosman won 17. The Mets did not have many good hitters, but they made the most of their chances while batting and played well in the field. Hodges was very good at guessing who would do well each game. He liked to give everyone a chance to play. At the end of the year, the Mets had won 100 games. They were the champions of the **NL East**.

After defeating the hard-hitting Atlanta Braves in the NLCS, the Mets faced the Baltimore Orioles in the World Series. The Orioles looked unbeatable. They had won nine more games, scored 147 more runs, and batted 23 points higher than the Mets.

The Mets lost the first game of the World Series. After that, they could do no wrong. New York beat Baltimore in five games. The hitting star of the series was Donn Clendenon, a 35-year-old first baseman who had almost retired earlier in the season.

In Game 4, Ron Swoboda made a great fielding play. He was known more for his bat than his glove. In Game 5, light-hitting Al Weis socked a long home run. He was known more for his glove than his bat. The team that had once been called the "Amazin' Mets" as a

LEFT: This 1969 trading card shows manager Gil Hodges.
ABOVE: New York City Mayor John Lindsay joins Tom Seaver as they celebrate a New York pennant.

joke shocked fans everywhere by becoming the champions of baseball.

Seventeen years later, the Mets won their second championship. In many ways, this victory was even more amazing. New York barely won the pennant, beating the Houston Astros in a wild 16-inning game in the NLCS. Then the Mets lost the first two games of the World Series to the Boston Red Sox—in Shea Stadium. No team had ever won a championship after losing the opening games on its home field.

Led by the pitching of Bob Ojeda and Ron Darling, plus the hitting of Lenny Dykstra and Gary Carter, New York battled back to tie the series. The Mets almost lost Game 6, but they made a remarkable comeback to win in the 10th inning. The team had to

come from behind again in Game 7. They won
8–5 on hits by Keith Hernandez, Ray Knight,
and Darryl Strawberry. For the second time in the
history of Shea Stadium, thousands of fans poured
onto the field to celebrate their team's championship. Knight
was named the series **Most Valuable Player (MVP)**.

LEFT: Lenny Dykstra rounds the bases after his home run to start
Game 3 of the 1986 World Series.
ABOVE: Ray Knight watches his winning hit in Game 7.

Go-To Guys

To be a true star in baseball, you need more than a quick bat and a strong arm. You have to be a "go-to guy"—someone the manager wants on the pitcher's mound or in the batter's box when it matters most. Fans of the Mets have had a lot to cheer about over the years, including these great stars …

THE PIONEERS

TOM SEAVER   Pitcher

• BORN: 11/17/1944 • PLAYED FOR TEAM: 1967 TO 1977 AND 1983

Tom Seaver was the team's first true star. He threw one fastball that hopped as it neared home plate, and another fastball that dipped. Batters did not know which to swing at until it was too late. "Tom Terrific" was an All-Star nine times with the Mets.

JERRY KOOSMAN   Pitcher

• BORN: 12/23/1942 • PLAYED FOR TEAM: 1967 TO 1978

Jerry Koosman had a good fastball, a great curve, and a "**cutter**" that caused a lot of broken bats. He was the pitching star of the 1969 World Series, beating the Orioles in Game 2 and Game 5.

KEITH HERNANDEZ   First Baseman

• BORN: 10/20/1953   • PLAYED FOR TEAM: 1983 TO 1989

Keith Hernandez was the best fielder in team history. He won the **Gold Glove** six times in the seven seasons he played for the Mets. Hernandez was also one of baseball's best **clutch** hitters.

DARRYL STRAWBERRY   Outfielder

• BORN: 3/12/1962   • PLAYED FOR TEAM: 1983 TO 1990

Darryl Strawberry was the first great hitter the Mets developed. He was a tall, graceful athlete with a beautiful swing. Strawberry was an All-Star in seven of his eight seasons with the Mets.

DWIGHT GOODEN   Pitcher

• BORN: 11/16/1964   • PLAYED FOR TEAM: 1984 TO 1994

At the age of 19, Dwight Gooden had baseball's best fastball and most amazing curve. In his first season, he struck out 276 batters. The next season, he led the NL in wins, strikeouts, and **earned run average (ERA)**.

GARY CARTER   Catcher

• BORN: 4/8/1954   • PLAYED FOR TEAM: 1985 TO 1989

The Mets needed an experienced catcher to work with their young pitchers in the mid-1980s. In 1985, they traded for Gary Carter, and one year later they were world champions.

LEFT: Jerry Koosmam
RIGHT: Darryl Strawberry

JOHN FRANCO   Pitcher

• BORN: 9/17/1960   • PLAYED FOR TEAM: 1990 TO 2004

John Franco's job was to slam the door on opponents in the ninth inning and close out the game for the Mets. He did this 276 times for the team and led the NL in **saves** twice while pitching in New York.

MIKE PIAZZA   Catcher

• BORN: 9/4/1968   • PLAYED FOR TEAM: 1998 TO 2005

Mike Piazza ranks among the greatest hitting catchers in baseball history. When the Mets won the pennant in 2000, he led all catchers in batting average, home runs, and **fielding percentage**. In 2004, he set a record for most home runs in a career by a catcher.

JOSE REYES   Shortstop

• BORN: 6/11/1983

• PLAYED FOR TEAM: 2003 TO 2011

New York fans started buzzing the first day Jose Reyes stepped on the field. His tremendous speed, powerful arm, and lively bat made him one of the best all-around shortstops in baseball. Reyes's bright smile made him one of the most popular Mets.

DAVID WRIGHT — Third Baseman

- BORN: 12/20/1982 • FIRST YEAR WITH TEAM: 2004

The Mets searched many years for a star to play third base for them. Their search ended when power-hitting David Wright joined the team. He developed into one of the NL's best hitters and won the Gold Glove for his fielding.

CARLOS BELTRAN — Outfielder

- BORN: : 4/24/1977 • PLAYED FOR TEAM: 2005 TO 2011

When the Mets signed Carlos Beltran, they were looking for a player with speed, power, and great defensive skills. Beltran did not disappoint them. In seven seasons with the Mets, he was an All-Star five times.

JON NIESE — Pitcher

- BORN: 10/27/1986 • FIRST YEAR WITH TEAM: 2008

Young left-handed pitchers who can master four different pitches are very rare. In 2010, Jon Niese had all of them working against the San Diego Padres. He allowed one hit and no walks in a brilliant 3–0 **shutout**. Niese was making only the 18th start of his **major-league** career!

LEFT: Jose Reyes
TOP RIGHT: David Wright   **BOTTOM RIGHT**: Jon Niese

23

The Mets have always liked to hire "hometown guys" to run the team. Their first manager, Casey Stengel, had been playing and managing in New York since 1912! The Mets found many more managers with ties to the New York area, including Wes Westrum, Yogi Berra, Joe Torre, Dallas Green, Bobby Valentine, and Willie Randolph.

One of the Mets' most successful managers was Davey Johnson. He led the team to its World Series championship in 1986. Johnson had never played for the Mets, but he spent a lot of time playing *against* them. He was a member of the Baltimore Orioles in 1969. They lost to New York in the World Series.

The Mets' greatest manager was another New York baseball legend. Gil Hodges had been an All-Star first baseman for the Brooklyn Dodgers in the 1950s. He loved New York and was heartbroken when the Dodgers moved to Los Angeles. When the Mets hired Hodges to manage their team in 1968, he was thrilled.

Hodges was a big, quiet man. When he spoke, players listened. When Hodges arrived in New York, the Mets thought of themselves

This 1970 trading card shows Gil Hodges. He led the Mets to their first championship in 1969.

Gil Hodges | MANAGER

as "loveable losers"—they didn't win often, but the fans adored them anyway. Hodges wanted his players to change their approach on the field and off of it. If they did all of the little things right, he promised, they could win a championship. In 1969, the Mets focused every day on pitching well, making smart plays, and getting key hits. At the end of the season, New York celebrated its first championship.

Hodges was the first Mets manager to show that the team could win by relying on strong pitching and defense. Every manager who followed him has tried to teach the players the same thing. Hodges passed away in 1972, but his spirit lives on every time the Mets take the field.

Game 6 of the 1986 World Series will forever be remembered as the most amazing day in Mets history. The Boston Red Sox led the series three games to two. As the bottom of the 10th inning began, the Mets were losing 5–3. There were only three outs left in their season.

Boston got two of those outs quickly. The Red Sox players inched closer to the top step of their dugout, waiting for that moment when they could run onto the field and start celebrating. But Gary Carter hit a single to keep New York's hopes alive. Then Kevin Mitchell singled. Ray Knight was next. He hit a single with two strikes, and Carter scored to make it 5–4.

Bob Stanley came into the game to pitch to Mookie Wilson. After getting two strikes on Wilson, he tried to put a little too much on a pitch, and it sailed way inside. Wilson jumped back to keep from being

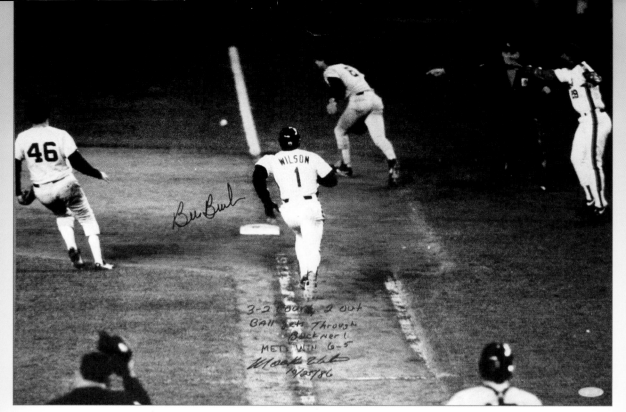

This photo autographed by Mookie Wilson and Bill Buckner shows their famous play from Game 6 of the 1986 World Series.

struck, and the ball rolled far from the catcher. Mitchell scored the tying run, and Knight ran to second base.

The next pitch was a good, low strike. Wilson pounded the ball into the ground, and it bounced toward first baseman Bill Buckner. Worried that the speedy Wilson might beat him to the base, Buckner took his eye off the ball for an instant—and it rolled under his glove and into the outfield. Knight scored all the way from second base to win the game! The Mets then beat Boston in Game 7 to capture the championship.

LEGEND HAS IT

WHO ONCE RAN THE BASES BACKWARDS FOR THE METS?

LEGEND HAS IT that Jimmy Piersall did. In 1963, Piersall joined the Mets with 99 career home runs. He decided to make number 100 a hit to remember. After blasting the ball over the fence against the Philadelphia Phillies, Piersall turned around and *backpedaled* his way around the bases. After rounding third base, he slid into home plate backwards.

ABOVE: Jimmy Piersall finishes his "backwards" run around the bases.

How did the Mets catch the Chicago Cubs in the 1969 pennant race?

LEGEND HAS IT that they had help from a cat. That September, with Chicago leading in the standings, the Cubs came to Shea Stadium to teach the young Mets a lesson. During the game, a black cat ran onto the field and headed straight toward Chicago's Ron Santo in the on-deck circle. Many people consider a black cat to be bad luck. Santo was the Cubs' leader—and their most *superstitious* player! When the Mets won the game, fans everywhere believed the black cat had cursed Chicago. The next day the Mets passed the Cubs in the standings, and they never looked back.

Which Met made one of baseball's greatest business deals?

LEGEND HAS IT that David Wright did. In 2006, a company in Queens asked him to endorse its product, Vitamin Water. Wright agreed to do so, in exchange for a tiny piece of ownership in the company. One year later, Coca-Cola bought Vitamin Water for more than $4 billion. Wright's "tiny piece" was suddenly worth close to $20 million—16 times what he made that year from playing baseball!

You can never count the Mets out. They have proved this again and again during their history. During the summer of 1973, everyone in baseball thought New York's season was over. On August 17, the Mets were in last place in the NL East. Five of their best players—Bud Harrelson, Jerry Grote, Cleon Jones, John Milner, and Willie Mays—had been hurt for much of the season.

When these players returned to the lineup, the Mets started winning. Slowly but surely, they began passing the clubs in front of them. Could the Mets do the impossible? Tug McGraw, the team's star relief pitcher, kept saying "You gotta believe." Soon, YOU GOTTA BELIEVE buttons and signs started popping up all over the city.

On September 27, New York fans woke up to find their team in first place. On October 1, Jon Matlack pitched a two-hitter against the Chicago Cubs to give the Mets the NL East title. They finished with 82 wins, one more than the second-place St. Louis Cardinals. The Mets went on to beat the Cincinnati Reds in the playoffs and win the pennant. In just a few weeks, New York had gone from worst to first!

Oh, that's cold! Willie Mays celebrates after the Mets win the 1973 pennant.

TEAM SPIRIT

There has always been something a little different about the fans who root for the Mets. They cheer like crazy when the team plays well, but they also can smile when the team does not. Mets fans know that baseball is a funny game, and that a good team can also have a bad day.

How long have Mets fans been looking at their team this way? This *tradition* started in the 1960s. Back then, the Mets did not have much talent. Their players tried hard and sometimes made amazing plays, but often they committed errors that were amazingly bad. Through it all, the fans have always inspired the players with the same cheer: *Let's Go Mets!* The 2011 season marked the 50th year that cheer has been heard in the team's ballpark.

LEFT: Team mascot Mr. Met listens to the fans cheer.
ABOVE: Mr. Met is also the star of this old stadium pennant.

TIMELINE

The Sporting News

JERRY KOOSMAN
Pitcher
METS

NATIONAL LEAGUE ALL-STARS

Jerry Koosman was an All-Star in 1969.

1962
The Mets play their first season.

1969
The Mets defeat the Baltimore Orioles in the World Series.

1964
Ron Hunt becomes the first Met to start in the **All-Star Game**.

1967
Tom Seaver is named **Rookie of the Year**.

1972
Jon Matlack is named Rookie of the Year.

NEW YORK Mets
FINAL YEAR BOOK 1964 50¢
SHEA STADIUM

This yearbook is from the 1964 season.

Jon Matlack

Yogi Berra

1973
Yogi Berra manages the Mets to the NL pennant.

1991
David Cone leads the NL in strikeouts for the second year in a row.

2006
The Mets play in the NLCS for the sixth time.

1986
The Mets win their second World Series.

2000
The Mets win their fourth pennant.

2011
Jose Reyes wins the NL batting title.

Darryl Strawberry led the 1986 Mets with 27 homers.

Jose Reyes

YOU BIG APE!

The most powerful hitter in Mets history was Dave Kingman. He slugged several 500-foot home runs and could hit balls over the fence on one-handed swings. Kingman's nickname was "Kong."

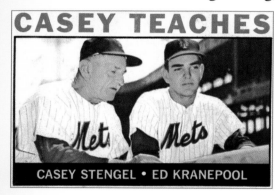
CASEY TEACHES
CASEY STENGEL • ED KRANEPOOL

THE GRADUATE

In 1962, 17-year-old Ed Kranepool graduated from high school in New York and was playing first base for the Mets a few weeks later.

PACIFIC HEIGHTS

The Mets have had great luck with players born in Hawaii, Japan, and Korea. Among the most successful were Sid Fernandez, Ron Darling, Benny Agbayani, Hideo Nomo, Kazuhisa Ishii, Kazuo Matsui, Masato Yoshii, Tsuyoshi Shinjo, and Ryota Igarashi.

ABOVE: Old-timer Casey Stengel talks hitting with teenager Ed Kranepool.
RIGHT: Rusty Staub

LAST LAUGHS

Pitcher Jerry Koosman got the final out of the Mets' first championship in 1969. Koosman was later traded for pitcher Jesse Orosco. Orosco got the last out of the Mets' second championship in 1980.

A MAN OF TASTE

Outfielder Rusty Staub was the best hitter on the 1973 Mets—and the best cook. Staub was a trained chef who owned his own restaurant.

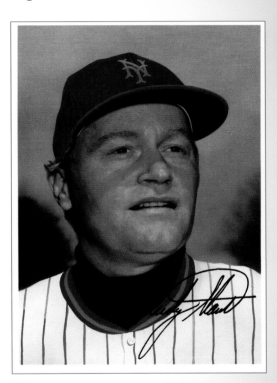

ME, MYSELF, AND I

In 1962, the Mets got catcher Harry Chiti in a trade with the Cleveland Indians for a "player to be named later." The player they named later was Chiti. That means he was traded for himself!

SLAMMIN' SUMMER

In July of 2006, the Mets tied a record by hitting six **grand slams** in a month. Carlos Beltran hit three, Jose Valentin hit two, and Cliff Floyd hit one.

"I like triples—when I hit a ball in the gap, all I think about is a triple."

▶ *JOSE REYES, ON THE SECRET TO GETTING THREE-BASE HITS*

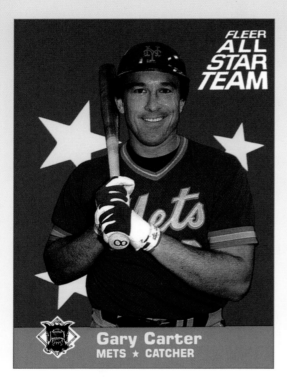

FLEER ALL STAR TEAM

Gary Carter
METS ★ CATCHER

"To me, that was the greatest accomplishment. Without a doubt, that was my biggest thrill."

▶ *GARY CARTER, ON WINNING THE 1986 WORLD SERIES WITH THE METS*

"I think experience is a great teacher."

▶ *BOBBY VALENTINE, ON THE IMPORTANCE OF LEARNING FROM MISTAKES*

"That kid can hit balls over buildings."

▶ *CASEY STENGEL, ON SLUGGER RON SWOBODA AFTER HE FIRST JOINED THE TEAM*

ABOVE: Gary Carter
RIGHT: David Wright leads the cheers from the Mets' dugout.

"You've got to have presence on the mound."

▶ **JOHAN SANTANA**, ON WHAT IT TAKES TO
BE A TEAM'S ACE PITCHER

"Good players feel the kind of love for the game that they did
when they were Little Leaguers."

▶ **TOM SEAVER**, ON WHAT INSPIRED HIM
DURING HIS PLAYING DAYS

"I think leadership is something that isn't shown by yelling and
screaming and throwing things."

▶ **DAVID WRIGHT**, ON LEADING BY EXAMPLE

GREAT DEBATES

People who root for the Mets love to compare their favorite moments, teams, and players. Some debates have been going on for years! How would you settle these classic baseball argum.ents?

THE 1969 METS WOULD BEAT THE 1986 METS IN A SERIES EVERY TIME ...

... because the 1969 Mets were pure magic—they could beat anyone! New York destroyed the Baltimore Orioles in the 1969 World Series, and many experts said the Orioles were one of the greatest teams in history. With a pitching staff led by Tom Seaver, Jerry Koosman, Gary Gentry (**LEFT**), Nolan Ryan, and Tug McGraw, the 1969 Mets would shut out the 1986 team in every game.

SERIOUSLY? NO TEAM WAS MORE MAGICAL THAN THE 1986 METS ...

... because they never gave up. Their comeback against the Boston Red Sox in Game 6 of the 1986 World Series was the greatest ever. The Mets were down to their last strike three times. They *rallied* to win that game and the next one, too. By the way, the 1986 Mets had great pitching, as well. The 1969 team couldn't touch Dwight Gooden, Ron Darling, Sid Fernandez, Roger McDowell, and Jesse Orosco.

TOMMIE AGEE MADE THE GREATEST CATCH IN METS HISTORY ...

... because his defense saved the 1969 World Series for New York. Agee played the outfield for five seasons for the Mets and earned a Gold Glove in 1970. He was at his best in Game 3 of the 1969 World Series. Agee made two amazing catches to save five runs. The Mets won the game, and the Orioles never recovered. Which of Agee's catches was the greatest? Who cares! They were both incredible!

OH, REALLY? NOTHING BEATS THE CATCH BY ENDY CHAVEZ IN GAME 7 OF THE 2006 NATIONAL LEAGUE CHAMPIONSHIP SERIES ...

... because he reached three feet over the left field fence to snatch a home run away from Scott Rolen of the St. Louis Cardinals. With the game tied 1–1, Chavez glided toward the wall, leaped high in the air, and robbed Rolen of the go-ahead homer. The team even made a bobblehead doll (RIGHT) of "The Catch" for fans the following season.

T he great Mets teams and players have left their marks on the record books. These are the "best of the best" …

Donn Clendenon

Ray Knight

METS AWARD WINNERS

WINNER	AWARD	YEAR
Tom Seaver	Rookie of the Year	1967
Tom Seaver	Cy Young Award*	1969
Donn Clendenon	World Series MVP	1969
Jon Matlack	Rookie of the Year	1972
Tom Seaver	Cy Young Award	1973
Tom Seaver	Cy Young Award	1975
Jon Matlack	All-Star Game co-MVP	1975
Darryl Strawberry	Rookie of the Year	1983
Dwight Gooden	Rookie of the Year	1984
Dwight Gooden	Cy Young Award	1985
Ray Knight	World Series MVP	1986
Mike Hampton	NLCS MVP	2000

The Cy Young award is given to the league's best pitcher each year.

WORLD CHAMPIONS

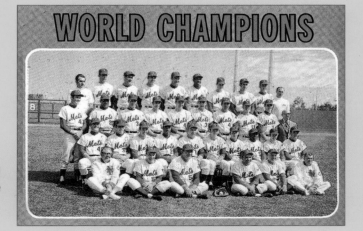

This trading card shows the 1969 Mets.

METS ACHIEVEMENTS

ACHIEVEMENT	YEAR
NL East Champions	1969
NL Pennant Winners	1969
World Series Champions	1969
NL East Champions	1973
NL Pennant Winners	1973
NL East Champions	1986
NL Pennant Winners	1986
World Series Champions	1986
NL East Champions	1988
NL Pennant Winners	2000
NL East Champions	2006

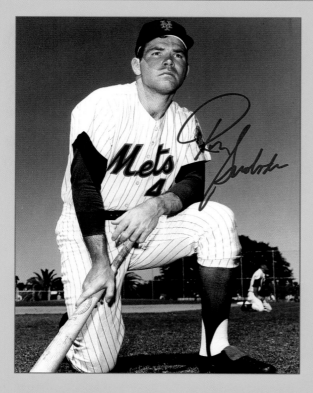

ABOVE: John Franco waves to the fans after the Mets win the 2000 pennant.
LEFT: Ron Swoboda, a star for the 1969 Mets, signed this photo.

PINPOINTS

The history of a baseball team is made up of many smaller stories. These stories take place all over the map—not just in the city a team calls "home." Match the pushpins on these maps to the **TEAM FACTS**, and you will begin to see the story of the Mets unfold!

TEAM FACTS

1 Flushing, New York—*The Mets have played here since 1964.*

2 Oakland, California—*The Mets played in the 1973 World Series here.*

3 Tampa, Florida—*Dwight Gooden was born here.*

4 Norfolk, Virginia—*David Wright was born here.*

5 Pendleton, Oregon—*Dave Kingman was born here.*

6 Houston, Texas—*The Mets won their third pennant here.*

7 Appleton, Minnesota—*Jerry Koosman was born here.*

8 Norristown, Pennsylvania—*Mike Piazza was born here.*

9 Honolulu, Hawaii—*Sid Fernandez was born here.*

10 Fukuoka, Japan—*Tsuyoshi Shinjo was born here.*

11 Tovar, Merida, Venezuela—*Johan Santana was born here.*

12 Villa Gonzalez, Dominican Republic—*Jose Reyes was born here.*

Tsuyoshi Shinjo

GLOSSARY

🧠 **ALL-STAR GAME**—Baseball's annual game featuring the best players from the American League and National League.

🧠 **AMERICAN LEAGUE (AL)**—One of baseball's two major leagues; the AL began play in 1901.

🧠 *BACKPEDALED*—Ran backwards.

🧠 **CLUTCH**—Describing a game situation with a lot of pressure.

🧠 **CUTTER**—A fastball that curves slightly to the right or left.

🧠 **EARNED RUN AVERAGE (ERA)**—A statistic that measures how many runs a pitcher gives up for every nine innings he pitches.

🧠 **FIELDING PERCENTAGE**—A statistic that measures a player's defensive ability.

🧠 **GOLD GLOVE**—An award given each year to baseball's best fielders.

🧠 **GRAND SLAMS**—Home runs with the bases loaded.

🧠 *LOGO*—A symbol or design that represents a company or team.

🧠 **MAJOR-LEAGUE**—The top level of professional baseball leagues. The AL and NL make up today's major leagues.

🧠 **MOST VALUABLE PLAYER (MVP)**—An award given each year to each league's top player; an MVP is also selected for the World Series and the All-Star Game.

🧠 **NATIONAL LEAGUE (NL)**—The older of the two major leagues; the NL began play in 1876.

🧠 **NATIONAL LEAGUE CHAMPIONSHIP SERIES (NLCS)**—The playoff series that has decided the NL pennant since 1969.

🧠 **NL EAST**—A group of National League teams that play in the eastern part of the country.

🧠 **PENNANT**—A league championship. The term comes from the triangular flag awarded to each season's champion, beginning in the 1870s.

🧠 *PINSTRIPE*—A design with thin stripes.

🧠 *RALLIED*—Improved suddenly.

🧠 **ROOKIE OF THE YEAR**—The annual award given to each league's best first-year player.

🧠 **SAVES**—A statistic that counts the number of times a relief pitcher finishes off a close victory for his team.

🧠 **SHUTOUT**—A game in which one team does not allow its opponent to score a run.

🧠 *SPARKLING*—Notable or eye-catching.

🧠 *STRATEGY*—A plan or method for succeeding.

🧠 *SUPERSTITIOUS*—Trusting in magic or luck.

🧠 *TRADITION*—A belief or custom that is handed down from generation to generation.

🧠 *VETERAN*—Possessing great experience.

🧠 **WORLD SERIES**—The world championship series played between the AL and NL pennant winners.

EXTRA INNINGS

TEAM SPIRIT introduces a great way to stay up to date with your team! Visit our **EXTRA INNINGS** link and get connected to the latest and greatest updates. **EXTRA INNINGS** serves as a young reader's ticket to an exclusive web page—with more stories, fun facts, team records, and photos of the Mets. Content is updated during and after each season. The **EXTRA INNINGS** feature also enables readers to send comments and letters to the author! Log onto:

www.norwoodhousepress.com/library.aspx

and click on the tab: **TEAM SPIRIT** to access **EXTRA INNINGS**.

Read all the books in the series to learn more about professional sports. For a complete listing of the baseball, basketball, football, and hockey teams in the **TEAM SPIRIT** series, visit our website at:

www.norwoodhousepress.com/library.aspx

ON THE ROAD

NEW YORK METS
123-01 Roosevelt Avenue
Flushing, New York 11368
(718) 507-6387
newyork.mets.mlb.com

**NATIONAL BASEBALL
HALL OF FAME AND MUSEUM**
25 Main Street
Cooperstown, New York 13326
(888) 425-5633
www.baseballhalloffame.org

ON THE BOOKSHELF

To learn more about the sport of baseball, look for these books at your library or bookstore:

• Augustyn, Adam (editor). *The Britannica Guide to Baseball*. New York, NY: Rosen Publishing, 2011.

• Dreier, David. *Baseball: How It Works*. North Mankato, MN: Capstone Press, 2010.

• Stewart, Mark. *Ultimate 10: Baseball*. New York, NY: Gareth Stevens Publishing, 2009.

ABOUT THE AUTHOR

MARK STEWART has written more than 50 books on baseball and over 150 sports books for kids. He grew up in New York City during the 1960s rooting for the Yankees and Mets, and was lucky enough to meet players from both teams. Mark comes from a family of writers. His grandfather was Sunday Editor of *The New York Times,* and his mother was Articles Editor of *Ladies' Home Journal* and *McCall's*. Mark has profiled hundreds of athletes over the past 25 years. He has also written several books about his native New York and New Jersey, his home today. Mark is a graduate of Duke University, with a degree in history. He lives and works in a home overlooking Sandy Hook, New Jersey. You can contact Mark through the Norwood House Press website.